SUMMARY

THINK

AND

GROW

RICH!

Napoleon Hill

Published and Distributed by
SOUND WISDOM
PO Box 310
Shippensburg, PA 17257-0310
717-530-2122

info@soundwisdom.com
www.soundwisdom.com

While efforts have been made to verify information contained in this publication, neither the author nor the publisher assumes any responsibility for errors, inaccuracies, or omissions. While this publication is chock-full of useful, practical information, it is not intended to be legal or accounting advice. All readers are advised to seek competent lawyers and accountants to follow laws and regulations that may apply to specific situations. The reader of this publication assumes responsibility for the use of the information. The author and publisher assume no responsibility or liability whatsoever on the behalf of the reader of this publication.

ISBN 13 TP: 978-1-64095-477-9
ISBN 13 eBook: 978-1-64095-478-6

For Worldwide Distribution, Printed in the USA
1 2 3 4 5 6 / 26 25 24 23

CONTENTS

Introduction

THIRTEEN STEPS TO RICHES

THINK AND GROW RICH presents a money-making formula based on the author's 25 years of research and in collaboration with more than 500 very distinguished people of great wealth and achievement.

Built on Napoleon Hill's famous Law of Success Philosophy, anyone who follows the wisdom shared in the book will have the knowledge to become a great leader in every and all endeavors including finance, education, management, politics, technology, arts/entertainment, business, government, medical/healthcare...you name it.

This book conveys the experience of more than 500 men of great wealth, who began at scratch, with nothing to give in return for riches except THOUGHTS, IDEAS, and ORGANIZED PLANS.

Here you have the entire philosophy of money-making. It describes thoughts, ideas, plans, what to do, and how to do it. You are offered complete instructions on how to sell your personal services as well as a perfect system of self-analysis that quickly discloses what has been standing between you and the "big money" in the past.

You may not need all that is to be found in the book—but you may need one idea, one plan, one suggestion to seriously launch you into the next level of success. Somewhere in the book you will find this needed stimulus.

There are thirteen essential principles to accumulate sufficient money to guarantee financial independence. But always remember, riches cannot always be measured in money. Money and material things are essential for freedom of body and mind, but the greatest of all riches can be evaluated only in terms of lasting friendships, harmonious family relationships, sympathy and understanding between business associates, and introspective harmony that brings peace of mind measurable only in spiritual values.

When you read, understand, and apply the Law of Success philosophy, you will be better prepared to attract and enjoy the higher, richer states and stages in life. Prepare yourself now to experience a changed life, which may help you not only to negotiate your way through life with harmony and understanding, but also for the accumulation of material riches in abundance.

As a final word of preparation before you begin the first chapter, may I offer one brief suggestion that provides the Andrew Carnegie secret—*All achievement and all earned riches have their beginning in an idea!* If you are ready for the secret, you already possess one half of it; therefore, you will readily recognize the other half the moment it reaches your mind.

DESIRE

The Starting Point of All Achievement

Every human being who reaches the age of understanding of the purpose of money wishes for it. Wishing does not bring riches. But desiring riches with a state of mind that becomes an obsession, then planning definite ways and means to acquire riches, and backing those plans with persistence that does not recognize failure, will bring riches.

The DESIRE for riches can be converted into a financial equivalent by following these six definite, practical steps:

1. Fix in your mind the exact amount of money you desire. It is not sufficient merely to say, "I want plenty of money." Have a definite amount in mind. (There is a psychological reason for definiteness that is described in a subsequent chapter.)

2. Determine exactly what you intend to give in return for the money you desire. (There is no such reality as "something for nothing.")

3. Establish a definite date when you intend to possess the money you desire.

4. Create a definite plan for carrying out your desire and begin at once— whether you are ready or not—to put this plan into action.

5. Write out a clear, concise statement of the amount of money you intend to acquire, name the time limit for

its acquisition, state what you intend to give in return for the money, and describe clearly the plan to accumulate it.

6. Read your written statement aloud, twice daily, once just before retiring at night, and once after rising in the morning. As you read, see and feel and believe yourself already in possession of the money.

It is important to follow the instructions described in these six steps. It is especially important to follow the instructions in step 6. You may complain that is impossible for you to "see yourself in possession of money" before you actually have it, but only those who become "money conscious" ever accumulate great riches.

These steps call for no "hard labor." No sacrifice. No great amount of education. But the successful application of these six steps does call for sufficient imagination to see and understand that accumulation of money cannot be left to chance, good fortune, and luck. All who have accumulated great fortunes first did a certain

amount of dreaming, hoping, wishing, DESIR-
ING, and PLANNING.

You may as well know, right here, that you can
never have riches in great quantities, UNLESS you
can work yourself into a white heat of DESIRE for
money and actually BELIEVE you will possess it.

Every great leader from the dawn of civilization
down to the present was a dreamer. Christianity
is the greatest potential power in the world today,
because its Founder was an intense dreamer who
had the vision and the imagination to see realities
in a mental and spiritual form before being transmuted into physical form.

In planning to acquire your share of the riches,
let no one influence you to scorn the dreamer. To
win the big stakes in this changed world, you must
catch the spirit of the great pioneers of the past,
whose dreams have given to civilization all that
it has of value, the spirit which serves as the life-
blood of our own country—your opportunity and
mine, to develop and market our talents.

If the thing you wish to do is right, and you
believe in it, go ahead and do it! Put your dream
across, and never mind what "they" say if you meet

with temporary defeat. *Every failure brings the seed of an equivalent success.*

President Abraham Lincoln dreamed of freedom for the slaves, put his dream into action, and barely missed living to see a united North and South translate his dream into reality. The Wright brothers dreamed of a machine that would fly through the air. Now we see evidence worldwide that they dreamed soundly. *Dreams are the seedlings of reality.* The world is filled with an abundance of OPPORTUNITY which the dreamers of the past never knew.

A BURNING DESIRE TO BE AND TO DO is the starting point from which the dreamer must take off. Dreams are not born of indifference, laziness, or lack of ambition.

Booker T. Washington was born in slavery, handicapped by race and color. Because he was tolerant, had an open mind at all times, on all subjects, and was a DREAMER, he left his impress for good on an entire race. Beethoven was deaf, John Milton was blind, but their names will last as long as time endures, because they dreamed and translated their dreams into organized thought.

Kindle anew in your mind the fire of hope, faith, courage, and tolerance. If you have these states of mind and a working knowledge of the principles described, all else you need will come to you, when you are READY for it.

I believe in the power of DESIRE backed by FAITH. I have seen this power lift people from lowly beginnings to places of power and wealth; I have seen it serve as a comeback after having been defeated in a hundred different ways.

How can you harness and use the power of DESIRE? All achievement, no matter what may be its nature or purpose, must begin with an intense, BURNING DESIRE for something definite.

Nature wraps up in the impulse of STRONG DESIRE "that something," which recognizes no such word as "impossible," and accepts no such reality as failure.

Step 2

FAITH

Visualization of and Belief in Attaining Your Desire

FAITH is the head chemist of the mind. When FAITH is blended with the vibration of thought, the subconscious mind instantly picks up the vibration, translates it into its spiritual equivalent, and transmits it to Infinite Intelligence, as in prayer.

The emotions of FAITH, LOVE, and SEX are the most powerful of all the major positive emotions. When the three are blended, they have the effect of "coloring" the vibration of thought in such a way that it instantly reaches the subconscious mind, where it is changed into its spiritual equivalent, the only form that induces a response from Infinite Intelligence.

FAITH is a state of mind that may be induced, or created, by affirmation or repeated instructions to the subconscious mind through the principle of auto-suggestion.

As an illustration, consider the purpose for why you may be reading this book. The object is, naturally, to acquire the ability to transmute the intangible thought impulse of DESIRE into its physical counterpart, money. By following the instructions, you may CONVINCE the subconscious mind that you believe you will receive what you ask for and it will act on that belief, which your subconscious mind passes back to you in the form of "FAITH," followed by definite plans for procuring what you desire.

The method for developing FAITH is extremely difficult to describe, almost as describing the color red to a blind man who has never seen color. Faith is a state of mind; and after you have mastered the thirteen principles, FAITH is a state of mind that develops voluntarily, through application and use of the principles.

Repetition of affirmation of orders to your subconscious mind is the only known method of voluntary development of the emotion of faith.

Perhaps the meaning may be made clearer through the following explanation as to the way people sometimes become criminals. Stated in the words of a famous criminologist, "When men first come into contact with crime, they abhor it. If they remain in contact with crime for a time, they become accustomed to it, and endure it. If they remain in contact with it long enough, they finally embrace it, and become influenced by it."

In connection with this, consider the statement, ALL THOUGHTS WHICH HAVE BEEN EMOTIONALIZED (given feeling), AND MIXED WITH FAITH, begin immediately to translate themselves into their physical equivalent or counterpart.

There are millions of people who BELIEVE themselves "doomed" to poverty and failure, because of some strange force over which they BELIEVE they have no control. They are the creators of their own "misfortunes," because of this negative BELIEF, which is picked up by the subconscious mind and translated into its physical equivalent.

Your BELIEF, or FAITH, determines the action of your subconscious mind. There is nothing to hinder you from "deceiving" your subconscious mind when giving it instructions through auto-suggestion.

Because it's true that people may become criminals by association with crime (a known fact), it is equally true that people may develop faith by voluntarily suggesting to the subconscious mind that they have faith. The mind comes, finally, to take on the nature of the influences that dominate it. Understand this truth, and you will know why it is essential for you to *encourage positive emotions* as dominating forces of your mind, and discourage and *eliminate negative emotions*.

Know that:

FAITH is the "eternal elixir" that gives life, power, and action to the impulse of thought! (That sentence is worth reading a second time, a third, and a fourth. It is worth reading aloud!)

FAITH is the starting point of all accumulation of riches!

FAITH is the basis of all "miracles" and all mysteries that can't be analyzed by the rules of science!

FAITH is the only known antidote for failure!

FAITH is the element, the "chemical" which, when mixed with prayer, gives us direct communication with Infinite Intelligence.

FAITH is the element that transforms the ordinary vibration of thought, created by our finite mind, into the spiritual equivalent.

FAITH is the only agency through which the cosmic force of Infinite Intelligence can be harnessed and used by people.

Each of these statements can be proved. The proof is simple and easily demonstrated. It is wrapped up in the principle of auto-suggestion. It is a well-known fact that we BELIEVE whatever we repeat to ourselves, whether true or false. If we repeat a lie over and over, we eventually accept the lie as truth. Moreover, we BELIEVE it to be the truth.

Everyone is what they believe they are, because of the DOMINATING THOUGHTS that we permit to occupy our mind. Thoughts that we deliberately place in our mind and encourage with sympathy, and mix any one or more of the emotions, constitute the motivating force that directs and controls our every movement, act, and deed!

Thoughts mixed with feelings of emotions constitute a magnetic force that attracts other similar or related thoughts.

A thought "magnetized" with emotion may be compared to a seed which, when planted in fertile soil, germinates, grows, and multiples itself over and over again, until what was originally one small seed becomes countless millions of seeds of the SAME BRAND!

RICHES begin in the form of THOUGHT! The amount is limited only by the person in whose mind the THOUGHT is put into motion. FAITH removes limitations! Remember this when you are ready to bargain with Life for whatever it is that you ask as your price for having passed this way.

AUTO-SUGGESTION

Influencing the Subconscious Mind

AUTO-SUGGESTION is suggestions and all self-administered stimuli that reach your mind through the five senses. Stated another way, auto-suggestion is self-suggestion. It is communication between the part of the mind where conscious thought takes place and serves as the seat of action for the subconscious mind.

Through the dominating thoughts we permit to remain in the conscious mind—whether negative or positive is immaterial—the principle of auto-suggestion voluntarily reaches the subconscious mind and influences it with these thoughts.

All sense impressions perceived through the five senses are stopped by the CONSCIOUS thinking mind, and may be either passed on to the subconscious mind or rejected, at will. The conscious faculty serves as an outer guard to the approach of the subconscious.

The fact that you are reading this book is an indication that you earnestly seek knowledge. If you are only a student, there is a chance that you may learn much that you did not know, but you will learn only by assuming an attitude of humility. If you choose to follow some of the instructions but neglect or refuse to follow others—you will fail! To get satisfactory results, you must follow ALL instructions in a spirit of FAITH.

The instructions in the six steps in the second chapter are summarized and blended with the principles covered by this chapter:

1. Go into some quiet spot (preferably in bed at night) where you will not be disturbed or interrupted, close your eyes, and repeat aloud (so you may hear your own words) the written statement of the amount of money you intend to accumulate, the time limit for its accumulation, and a description of the service or merchandise you intend to give in return for the money. As you carry out these instructions, see yourself already in possession of the money.

    For example: Suppose you intend to accumulate $50,000 by the first of January, five years from now, and that you intend to be a salesman in return for the money. Your written statement of your purpose should be similar to the following: By the first day of January YEAR, I will have in my possession $50,000 that will come to me in various amounts from time to time during the interim. In return for this money I will give my most efficient service, rendering the fullest possible quantity, and the best possible quality of service as a salesperson (describe the service or merchandise you intend to sell). I believe I will have this money in my possession. My faith is so strong that I can now see this money before my eyes. I can touch it with my hands. It is now awaiting transfer to me at the time and in the proportion that I deliver the service I will give in return for it. I am waiting for a plan to accumulate this money, and I will follow that plan when it is received.

2. Repeat this program night and morning until you can see, in your imagination, the money you intend to accumulate.

3. Place a written copy for your statement where you can see it night and morning, and read it just before retiring and upon rising until it has been memorized.

Remember, as you carry out these instructions you are applying the principle of auto-suggestion for the purpose of giving orders to your subconscious mind. Remember also that your subconscious mind will act ONLY on instructions that are emotionalized and handed over to it with "feeling." FAITH is the strongest and most productive of the emotions. Follow the instructions given in the chapter on FAITH.

These instructions may, at first, seem abstract. Do not let this disturb you. Follow the instructions, no matter how abstract or impractical they may first appear to be. The time will soon come, if you do as you have been instructed, in spirit as well as in act, when a whole new universe of power will unfold to you.

Skepticism, in connection will ALL new ideas, is characteristic of all human beings. But if you follow the instructions outlined, your skepticism will soon be replaced by belief, and this in turn will soon become crystallized into ABSOLUTE FAITH. Then you will have arrived at the point where you may truly say, "I am the master of my fate. I am the captain of my soul!"

Humans may become the masters of themselves and of their environment because they have the POWER TO INFLUENCE THEIR OWN SUBCONSCIOUS MIND, and through it, gain the cooperation of Infinite Intelligence.

The wisdom in this chapter represents the keystone to the arch of the Law of Success philosophy. The instructions contained in this chapter must be understood and APPLIED WITH PERSISTENCE, if you want to succeed in converting desire into money.

The actual performance of transmuting DESIRE into money involves the use of auto-suggestion to reach and influence the subconscious mind. The other principles are simply tools to apply auto-suggestion. Keep this thought in mind and you will, at all times, be conscious of the important part the principle of auto-suggestion is to play in your efforts to accumulate money through the methods described in this abridged edition—and in even more greater detail in the original book, *Think and Grow Rich*.

Carry out these instructions with the FAITH of a child. The author has been most careful to provide practical instructions in a sincere desire to be helpful.

SPECIALIZED KNOWLEDGE

Personal Experiences or Observations

There are two kinds of knowledge. One is general, the other is specialized. General knowledge, no matter how great in quantity or variety it may be, is of little use in accumulating money. The faculties of the great universities possess, in the aggregate, practically every form of general knowledge known to civilization. Yet, most of the professors have but little or no money. They specialize on teaching knowledge; they don't specialize on the organization or the use of knowledge.

KNOWLEDGE will not attract money, unless it is organized and intelligently directed through practical PLANS OF ACTION, to the DEFINITE END. Lack of understanding this fact has been the source of confusion to millions of people who falsely believe that "knowledge is power." It is nothing of the sort! Knowledge is only potential power.

Before you can be sure of your ability to transmute DESIRE into its monetary equivalent, you will require SPECIALIZED KNOWLEDGE of the service, merchandise, or profession you intend to offer in return for fortune. Perhaps you may need much more specialized knowledge than you have the ability or the inclination to acquire, and if this should be true, you may bridge your weakness through the aid of your "Master Mind" group.

SPECIALIZED KNOWLEDGE is among the most plentiful and the cheapest forms of service which may be had! If you doubt this, consult the payroll of any university.

First of all, decide the sort of specialized knowledge you require and the purpose it is needed. To a large extent your major purpose in life, your goal, will help determine what knowledge you need. With this question settled, your next move requires that you have accurate information concerning dependable sources of knowledge. The more important of these are:

- Your own experience and education

- Experience and education available through cooperation of others (Master Mind Alliance)

- Colleges and universities (Online educational services as well)

- Public Libraries and the Internet (Books and periodicals where can be found all known knowledge)

- Special Training Courses (Night schools and home study schools)

As knowledge is acquired, it must be organized and put into use, for a definite purpose, through practical plans. Knowledge has no value except what can be gained from its application toward some worthy end. This is one reason why college degrees are not valued more highly. They represent nothing but miscellaneous knowledge.

If you contemplate acquiring additional schooling, first determine the purpose for that knowledge, then research where this sort of knowledge can be obtained from reliable sources.

Successful people in all callings never stop acquiring specialized knowledge related to their major purpose, business, or profession. Those who are not successful usually make the mistake of believing that the knowledge acquiring period ends when they finish school. The truth is that schooling does little more than provide practical knowledge. The home study method of training is especially suited to the needs of employed people who find, after leaving school, that they must acquire additional specialized knowledge, but cannot spare the time to go back to school.

Anything acquired without effort and without cost is generally unappreciated. The SELF-DIS-CIPLINE we receive from a definite program of specialized study makes up, to some extent, for the wasted opportunity when knowledge was available without cost at public schools.

Correspondence (online) schools are highly organized business institutions and tuition fees are reasonable. Being asked to pay, whether the student makes good grades or poor, causes students to follow through with the course. Credible correspondence schools constitute training on DECISION, PROMPTNESS, ACTION and THE HABIT OF FINISHING what was started.

There is no fixed price for sound IDEAS! In back of all IDEAS is specialized knowledge. Unfortunately, for those who do not find riches in abundance, specialized knowledge is more abundant and more easily acquired than IDEAS. Because of this very truth, there is a universal demand and an ever-increasing opportunity for the person capable of helping men and women to sell their personal services advantageously. Capability means IMAGINATION, the one quality needed to combine specialized knowledge with IDEAS, in the form of ORGANIZED PLANS designed to yield riches.

If you have IMAGINATION this chapter may present you with an idea sufficient to serve as the beginning of the riches you desire. Remember, the

IDEA is the main thing. Specialized knowledge may be found just around the corner—any corner!

IMAGINATION

The Workshop of the Mind

Your imagination is literally the workshop where plans are created. The impulse, the DESIRE, is given shape, form, and ACTION through the aid of the imaginative faculty of the mind. It has been said that humans can create anything they can imagine.

Of all the ages of civilization, this is the most favorable for the development of the imagination, because it is an age of rapid change. At every turn we can contact stimuli that develop the imagination.

The imaginative faculty functions in two forms—synthetic imagination and creative imagination.

Synthetic Imagination: Through synthetic imagination, you may arrange old concepts, ideas, or plans into new combinations. Synthetic imagination creates nothing; it merely works with the material of experience, education, and observation that it is fed. It is used most by an inventor, with the exception of the "genius" who draws on the creative imagination, when the problem cannot be solved through synthetic imagination.

Creative Imagination: Through creative imagination, the human finite mind has direct communication with Infinite Intelligence. This is when "hunches" and "inspirations" are received, and all basic or new ideas are handed over to people.

Keep in mind as you follow these principles that the entire story of how we convert DESIRE into money cannot be told in one statement. The story is complete only when we have MASTERED, ASSIMILATED, and BEGUN TO MAKE USE of all the principles.

The great leaders of business, industry, finance, and the great artists, musicians, poets, and writers became great because they developed their creative imagination. Both the synthetic and creative imagination become more alert with use, just as any muscle or organ of the body develops through use. Your imaginative faculty may have become weak through inaction. It can be revived and made alert through USE.

Detailed instructions for the building of plans have been given in almost every chapter of the original *Think and Grow Rich* book. Carry out the instructions best suited to your needs and reduce your plan to writing, if you have not already done so. *The moment you complete your plan, you will have DEFINITELY given concrete form to the intangible DESIRE.* Read that sentence once more. Read it aloud, very slowly, and as you do so, remember that you have now actually TAKEN THE FIRST of a series of steps that enable you to convert the thought into its physical counterpart.

DESIRE is thought impulse! Thought impulses are forms of energy. When you begin with the thought impulse, DESIRE, to accumulate money, you are drafting into your service the same "stuff" that Nature used in creating this earth and every material form in the universe, including the body and brain where the thought impulses function.

As far as science has been able to determine, the entire universe consists of two elements—matter and energy. Through the combination of energy and matter everything has been created, from the largest star floating in the air down to and including humans themselves.

You are now engaged in the task of trying to profit by Nature's method. You are sincerely and earnestly trying to adapt yourself to Nature's laws by endeavoring to convert DESIRE into its physical or monetary equivalent. YOU CAN DO IT! IT HAS BEEN DONE BEFORE!

Nature advertises this "secret" in the terms of biology, in the conversion of a tiny cell, so small that it may be lost on the point of a pin, into the HUMAN BEING now reading this line. The conversion of desire into its physical equivalent is, certainly, no more miraculous!

The principles that follow open the way for understanding your imagination. Assimilate what you understand as you read this philosophy for the first time. Then when you reread and study it, you will discover that something has happened to clarify it and give you a broader understanding of the whole. Above all, DO NOT STOP nor hesitate in your study of these principles until you have read this book at least THREE times—then you are encouraged to read the original book that delves into these principles deeply, accompanied with true life stories and ideas that yielded huge fortunes.

Millions of people go through life hoping for favorable "breaks." Perhaps a break can get someone an opportunity, but the safest plan is not to depend on luck. My favorable break came through Andrew Carnegie, one of the richest men in American history. But what about my DETERMINATION, DEFINITENESS OF PURPOSE, and the DESIRE TO ATTAIN THE GOAL, and the PERSISTENT EFFORT OF TWENTY-FIVE YEARS? It was no ordinary DESIRE that survived disappointment, discouragement, temporary defeat, criticism, and the constant reminding of "waste of time." It was a BURNING DESIRE! An OBSESSION!

Ideas are like that. First you give life and action and guidance to ideas, then they take on a power of their own and sweep aside all opposition. Ideas are intangible forces, but they have more power than the physical brains that give birth to them. They have the power to live on after the brain that creates them has returned to dust.

For example, take the power of Christianity. That began with a simple idea, born in the brain of Christ. Its chief tenet was, "do unto others as you would have others do unto you." Christ has gone back to the source from whence He came, but His IDEA goes marching on. Someday it may grow up and come into its own, then it will have fulfilled Christ's deepest DESIRE. The IDEA has been developing for only two thousand years. Give it time!

ORGANIZED PLANNING

The Transformation of Desire into Action

YOU have learned so far that everything anyone has ever created or acquired began in the form of DESIRE; that desire was taken from the abstract to the concrete, into the workshop of the IMAGINATION where PLANS for its transition were created and organized.

In Step 1, you were instructed to take six definite, practical steps as your first move in translating the desire for money into its monetary equivalent. One of these steps is the formation of a DEFINITE, practical plan, or plans.

How to build practical plans:

1. Ally yourself with a group of as many people as you may need for the creation and carrying out of your plan for the accumulation of money— making use of the "Master Mind" principle described in a later step. (Compliance with this instruction is absolutely essential. Do not neglect it.)

2. Before forming your Master Mind alliance, decide what advantages and benefits you may offer the individual members of your group in return for their cooperation. No one will work indefinitely without some form of compensation. No intelligent person will either request or expect another to work without adequate compensation, although

this may not always be in the form of money.

3. Arrange to meet with the members of your Master Mind group at least twice a week, more often if possible, until you have jointly perfected the necessary plan for the accumulation of money.

4. Maintain PERFECT HARMONY between yourself and every member of your Master Mind group. If you fail to carry out this instruction to the letter, you may expect to meet with failure. The Master Mind principle cannot succeed where PERFECT HARMONY does not prevail.

Keep in mind these facts:

1. You are engaged in an undertaking of major importance to you. To be sure of success you must have faultless plans.

2. You must have the advantage of the experience, education, native ability, and imagination of other

minds. This is a fact proven by every person who has accumulated a great fortune.

No individual has sufficient experience, education, native ability, and knowledge to insure the accumulation of a great fortune without the cooperation of other people. Every plan you adopt in your endeavor to accumulate wealth should be the joint creation between you and every member of your Master Mind group. You may originate your own plans, either in whole or in part, but have your Master Mind group review and approve each plan.

If the first plan you adopt doesn't work successfully, replace it with a new plan. If the new plan fails to work, replace it in turn with still another, and so on, until you find a plan which DOES WORK. Right here is the point at which the majority of people meet with failure, because of their lack of PERSISTENCE in creating new plans to replace ones that fail.

Temporary defeat should mean only one thing: the certain knowledge that there is something wrong with your plan. Millions of people go through life in misery and poverty because they lack a sound plan through which to accumulate a fortune.

Your achievement can be no greater than your PLANS are sound. That may seem to be an axiomatic statement, but it is true. No one is ever whipped until he QUITS—in his own mind.

This fact will be repeated many times, because it is so easy to bail out at the first sign of defeat.

No follower of this philosophy can reasonably expect to accumulate a fortune without experiencing temporary defeat.

When defeat comes, accept it as a signal that your plans are not sound, rebuild those plans, and set sail once more toward your coveted goal. If you give up before your goal has been reached, you are a quitter. A QUITTER NEVER WINS—AND—A WINNER NEVER QUITS. Lift this sentence out, write it on a piece of paper in letters an inch high, and place it where you will see it every night before you go to sleep, and every morning before you go to work.

When you begin to select members for your Master Mind group, select those who do not take defeat seriously. Some people foolishly believe that only MONEY can make money. This is not true! DESIRE, transmuted into its monetary equivalent through these thirteen principles, is how money is "made." Money is actually nothing but inert matter. It cannot move, think, or talk—but it can "hear" when someone who DESIRES it calls it to come!

The original book explains in detail: sale of services plan; leadership attributes; causes of leadership failures; when and how to apply for positions; media marketing; application "brief"; obtaining the exact position you desire; where and how to accumulate riches; and other important information.

Step 7

DECISION

Mastering Procrastination

Analysis of over 25,000 men and women who had experienced failure disclosed the fact that LACK OF DECISION was near the head of the list of the 30 major causes of FAILURE. This is no mere statement of a theory—it's a fact.

PROCRASTINATION, the opposite of DECISION, is a common enemy that practically every person must conquer. You will have an opportunity to test your capacity to reach quick and definite DECISIONS when you finish reading this book, and are ready to begin putting into ACTION the principles it describes.

Analysis of several hundred people who had accumulated fortunes disclosed that each had the habit of REACHING DECISIONS PROMPTLY, and of changing these decisions SLOWLY, if they were changed.

The majority of people who fail to accumulate money sufficient for their needs are generally easily influenced by the "opinions" of others. They allow newspapers and "gossiping" neighbors to do their "thinking" for them. Opinions are the cheapest commodities on earth. If you are influenced by opinions when you reach DECISIONS, you will not succeed in any undertaking, much less transmuting YOUR OWN DESIRE into money.

If you are influenced by the opinions of others, you will have no DESIRE of your own.

Keep your own counsel when you begin to put into practice the principles described here, by reaching your own decisions and following them. Take no one into your confidence, EXCEPT the members of your Master Mind group, and be very sure in your selection of this group. Choose ONLY those who are in COMPLETE SYMPATHY AND HARMONY WITH YOUR PURPOSE.

Close friends and relatives, while not meaning to do so, often handicap us through opinions and sometimes through ridicule, which is meant to be humorous. Countless men and women carry inferiority complexes all through life because some well-meaning but ignorant person destroyed their confidence through opinions or ridicule.

You have a brain and mind of your own. USE IT, and reach your own decisions. If you need facts or information from other people to enable you to reach decisions—as you probably will in many instances—acquire the facts or secure the information you need quietly, without disclosing your purpose.

Keep in mind the fact that everyone with whom you associate is, like yourself, seeking the opportunity to accumulate money. If you talk about your plans too freely, you may be surprised that someone else has beaten you to your goal by PUTTING YOUR PLANS INTO ACTION AHEAD OF YOU.

In your search for the secret of the method, do not look for a miracle, because you will not find it. You will find only the eternal laws of Nature. These laws are available to every person who has the FAITH and the COURAGE to use them. They may be used to bring freedom to a nation, or to accumulate riches. There is no charge save the time necessary to understand and appropriate them.

Those who reach DECISIONS promptly and definitely know what they want, and generally get it. The leaders in every walk of life DECIDE quickly, and firmly. That is the major reason why they are leaders. The world has the habit of making room for the man whose words and actions show that he knows where he is going.

INDECISION is a habit that usually begins in youth. The habit takes on permanency as the youth goes through grade school, high school, and even through college, without DEFINITENESS OF PURPOSE. The major weakness of all educational systems is that they neither teach nor encourage the habit of DEFINITE DECISION.

DEFINITENESS OF DECISION always requires courage, sometimes very great courage. The fifty-six men who signed the Declaration of Independence staked their lives on the DECISION to affix their signatures to that document.

People who reach a DEFINITE DECISION to procure the particular job, and make life pay the price asked, do not stake their lives on that decision; they stake their ECONOMIC FREE-DOM. Financial independence, riches, desirable business and professional positions are not within reach of the person who neglects or refuses to EXPECT, PLAN, and DEMAND these things.

Step 8

PERSISTENCE

Sustained Effort Is Necessary to Induce Faith

PERSISTENCE is an essential factor when converting DESIRE into its monetary equivalent. The basis of persistence is the POWER OF WILL. Willpower and desire, when properly combined, make an irresistible pair. Whoever accumulates great fortunes is generally known as cold-blooded, and sometimes ruthless. Often they are misunderstood. What they have is willpower, which they mix with persistence and desire to insure the attainment of their objectives.

The majority of people are ready to throw their aims and purposes overboard, and give up at the first sign of opposition or misfortune. A few carry on DESPITE all opposition, until they attain their goal.

There may be no heroic connotation to the word "persistence," but the quality is to the character of person what carbon is to steel. The building of a fortune, generally, involves the application of the entire thirteen factors of this philosophy. These principles must be understood; they must be applied with PERSISTENCE by all who accumulate money.

If you are following this book with the intention of applying the knowledge it conveys, your first test as to your PERSISTENCE will come when you begin to follow the six steps described in Step 1. Unless you are one of the two out of every hundred who already have a DEFINITE GOAL you are aiming toward, and a DEFINITE PLAN for its attainment, you may read the instructions and then continue with your daily routine and never comply with those instructions.

THERE IS NO SUBSTITUTE FOR PER-SISTENCE! It cannot be supplanted by any other quality! Remember this, and it will hearten you, in the beginning, when the going may seem difficult and slow.

Every failure brings the seed of an equivalent advantage.

There are exceptions to this rule; a few people know from experience the soundness of persistence. They are those who have not accepted defeat as being anything more than temporary. They are the ones whose DESIRES are so PERSISTENTLY APPLIED that defeat is finally changed into victory. We who stand on the sidelines of life see the overwhelmingly large number who go down in defeat, never to rise again. We see the few who take the punishment of defeat as an urge to greater effort. These, fortunately, never learn to accept life's reverse gear.

But what we DO NOT SEE, what most of us never suspect of existing, is the silent but irresistible POWER that comes to the rescue of those who fight on in the face of discouragement. If we speak of this power at all we call it PERSISTENCE, and let it go at that. If someone does not possess PERSISTENCE, the person does not achieve noteworthy success in any calling.

Persistence is a state of mind, therefore it can be cultivated. Like all states of mind, persistence is based on definite causes, among them:

1. DEFINITENESS OF PURPOSE. Knowing what you want is the first and perhaps the most important step toward the development of persistence. A strong motive forces you to surmount many difficulties.

2. DESIRE. It is comparatively easy to acquire and to maintain persistence in pursuing the object of intense desire.

3. SELF-RELIANCE. Belief in your ability to carry out a plan encourages you to follow the plan through with persistence. (Self-reliance can be developed through the principle described in Step 3, auto-suggestion.)

4. DEFINITENESS OF PLANS. Organized plans encourage persistence,

even though a plan may be weak and entirely impractical.

5. ACCURATE KNOWLEDGE. Knowing that your plans are sound, based on experience or observation, encourages persistence; "guessing" rather than "knowing" destroys persistence.

6 COOPERATION. Sympathy, understanding, and harmonious cooperation with others tend to develop persistence.

7 WILLPOWER. The habit of concentrating your thoughts on building plans for the attainment of a definite purpose leads to persistence.

8 HABIT. Persistence is the direct result of habit. The mind absorbs and becomes part of the daily experiences on which it feeds. Fear, the worst of all enemies, can be effectively cured by forced repetition of acts of courage. Everyone who has seen active service in war knows this.

Before leaving the subject of PERSISTENCE, take inventory of yourself and determine if you are lacking in this essential quality. Measure yourself courageously, point by point, and see how many of the eight factors of persistence you lack. The analysis may lead to discoveries that will give you a new outlook.

THE MASTER MIND

Powerful Driving Force

The "Master Mind" may be defined as: "Coordination of knowledge and effort, in a spirit of harmony, between two or more people, for the attainment of a definite purpose."

No one has great power without the Master Mind. In a preceding Step, instructions were given for the creation of PLANS for the purpose of translating DESIRE into its monetary equivalent. If you carry out these instructions with PERSISTENCE and intelligence, and use discrimination in the selection of your Master Mind group, your objective is half-way reached, even before you begin to recognize it.

There are two characteristics of the Master Mind principle: one is economic and the other psychic. The *economic* feature is obvious. Economic advantages may be created by anyone who surrounds themselves with the advice, counsel, and personal cooperation of a group who are willing to lend wholehearted aid, in a spirit of PERFECT HARMONY. This form of cooperative alliance has been the basis of nearly every great fortune. Your understanding of this great truth may definitely determine your financial status.

The *psychic* phase of the Master Mind principle is much more abstract, much more difficult to comprehend, because it refers to the spiritual forces with which the human race, as a whole, is not well acquainted.

Keep in mind the fact that there are only two known elements in the whole universe—energy and matter. It is a well-known fact that matter may be broken down into units of molecules, atoms, and electrons. There are units of matter that may be isolated, separated, and analyzed.

Likewise, there are units of energy. The human mind is a form of energy, part of it being spiritual in nature. When the minds of two people are coordinated in a SPIRIT OF HARMONY, the spiritual units of energy of each mind form an affinity, which constitutes the psychic phase of the Master Mind.

The Master Mind principle, or rather the economic feature of it, was first called to my attention by Mr. Andrew Carnegie. Discovery of this principle was responsible for the choice of my life's work. Carnegie's Master Mind group consisted of approximately fifty men, for the DEFINITE PURPOSE of manufacturing and marketing steel. He attributed his entire fortune to the POWER he accumulated through this Master Mind.

Analyze the record of anyone who has accumulated a great fortune, and many have either consciously or unconsciously employed the Master Mind principle. I believe that great power can be accumulated through no other principle.

ENERGY is Nature's universal set of building blocks, out of which is built every material thing in the universe, including humans and every form of animal and vegetable life. Through a process that only Nature completely understands, energy is translated into matter.

Nature's building blocks are available to us in the energy involved in THINKING! Our brain may be compared to an electric battery. It absorbs energy from the ether, which permeates every atom of matter, and fills the entire universe.

It is a well-known fact that a group of electric batteries will provide more energy than a single battery. It is also a well-known fact that an individual battery will provide energy in proportion to the number and capacity of the cells it contains.

The brain functions in a similar fashion. This accounts for the fact that some brains are more efficient than others, and leads to this significant statement—a group of brains coordinated (or connected) in a spirit of harmony will provide more thought-energy than a single brain.

Through this metaphor it becomes immediately obvious that the Master Mind principle holds the secret of the POWER wielded by those who surround themselves with brainy people.

The chief sources from which POWER may be attained is headed by INFINITE INTELLIGENCE. When two or more people coordinate in a spirit of HARMONY and work toward a definite objective, they place themselves a position, through that alliance, to absorb power directly from the great universal storehouse of Infinite Intelligence. This is the greatest of all sources of POWER. It is the source to which the genius turns. It is the source to which every great leader turns, whether or not conscious of the fact.

In subsequent Steps, the most efficient methods of contacting Infinite Intelligence will be adequately described.

This is not a course on religion. No fundamental principle described in this book should be interpreted as being intended to interfere either directly or indirectly with anyone's religious habits. This abridged edition and the original book, *Think and Grow Rich*, have been confined, exclusively, to instructing the reader how to transmute the DEFINITE PURPOSE OF DESIRE FOR MONEY into its monetary equivalent.

Read, THINK, and meditate as you read. Soon the entire subject will unfold, and you will see it in perspective. You are now seeing the detail of the individual Steps.

Step 10

THE MYSTERY OF SEX TRANSMUTATION

THE MEANING OF THE word "transmute" is, in simple language, "the changing or transferring of one element or form of energy into another." The emotion of sex brings into being a state of mind.

Because of ignorance on the subject, this state of mind is generally associated with the physical, and because of improper influences, to which most people have been subjected in acquiring knowledge of sex, things essentially physical have highly biased the mind.

The emotion of sex has back of it the possibility of three constructive potentialities:

1. The perpetuation of humankind

2. The maintenance of health; as a therapeutic agency, it has no equal

3. The transformation of mediocrity into genius through transmutation

Sex transmutation is simple and easily explained. It means the switching of the mind from thoughts of physical expression to thoughts of some other nature.

Sexual desire is the most powerful of human desires. When driven by this desire, men develop keenness of imagination, courage, willpower, persistence, and creative ability unknown to them at other times. So strong and impelling is the desire for sexual contact that men freely run the risk of life and reputation to indulge it. When harnessed, and redirected along other lines, this motivating force maintains all of its attributes of keenness of imagination, courage, etc., which may be used as powerful creative forces in literature, art, or in any other profession or calling, including, of course, the accumulation of riches.

The transmutation of sex energy calls for the exercise of willpower, to be sure, but the reward is worth the effort. The desire for sexual expression is inborn and natural. The desire cannot and should not be submerged or eliminated. But it should be given an outlet through forms of expression that enrich the body, mind, and spirit. If not given this form of outlet, through transmutation, it will seek outlets through purely physical channels.

Fortunate, indeed, is the person who has discovered how to give sex emotion an outlet through some form of creative effort, for by that discovery a person can be lifted to the status of a genius.

The emotion of sex is an "irresistible force," against which there can be no such opposition as an "immovable body." The emotion of sex contains the secret of creative ability.

The human mind responds to stimuli, through which it may be "keyed up" to high rates of vibration, known as enthusiasm, creative imagination, intense desire, etc. The stimuli to which the mind responds most freely are:

1. The desire for sex expression
2. Love

3. A burning desire for fame, power, or financial gain, MONEY

4. Music

5. Friendship between either those of the same sex or those of the opposite sex

6. A Master Mind alliance based on the harmony of two or more people who ally themselves for spiritual or temporal advancement

7. Mutual suffering, such as that experienced by people who are persecuted

8. Auto-suggestion

9. Fear

10. Narcotics and alcohol

The desire for sex expression comes at the head of the list of stimuli, which most effectively "step up" the vibrations of the mind and start the "wheels" of physical action. Eight of these stimuli are natural and constructive. Two are destructive. The list is here presented for the purpose of enabling you to make a comparative study of the major sources of mind stimulation.

From this study, it is readily seen that the emotion of sex is, by great odds, the most intense and powerful of all mind stimuli. This comparison is necessary as a foundation for proof of the statement that transmutation of sex energy may lift one to the status of a genius.

The road to genius consists of the development, control, and use of sex, love, and romance.

Briefly, the process may be stated as follows: Encourage the presence of these emotions as the dominating thoughts in one's mind, and discourage the presence of all the destructive emotions. The mind is a creature of habit. It thrives on the dominating thoughts fed it. Through the faculty of willpower, one may discourage the presence of any emotion, and encourage the presence of any other.

Control of the mind, through the power of will, is not difficult. Control comes from persistence, and habit. The secret of control lies in understanding the process of transmutation. When any negative emotion presents itself in our mind, it can be transmuted into a positive, or constructive, emotion by the simple procedure of changing our thoughts.

The emotions of love and sex leave their unmistakable marks. The emotion of love brings out and develops the artistic and the aesthetic nature of humanity. It leaves its impress on our very soul, even after the fire has been subdued by time and circumstance.

Much more on this topic is shared in the original book, *Think and Grow Rich*.

Step 11

THE SUBCONSCIOUS MIND

The Connecting Link

THE SUBCONSCIOUS MIND consists of a field of consciousness in which every impulse of thought that reaches the objective mind through any of the five senses is classified and recorded, and from which thoughts may be recalled or withdrawn.

The subconscious mind receives, and files, sense impressions or thoughts, regardless of their nature. You may VOLUNTARILY plant in your subconscious mind any plan, thought, or purpose you desire to translate into its physical or monetary equivalent. The subconscious acts first on the dominating desires that have been mixed with emotional feeling, such as faith.

THE SUBCONSCIOUS MIND WORKS DAY AND NIGHT. Through a method of procedure unknown to us, the subconscious mind draws on the forces of Infinite Intelligence for the power to voluntarily transmute our desires into their physical equivalent, making use always of the most practical media.

You cannot entirely control your subconscious mind, but you can voluntarily hand over to it any plan, desire, or purpose you wish to transform into concrete form. Read, again, instructions for using the subconscious mind in Step 3.

There is evidence to support the belief that the subconscious mind is the connecting link between the human finite mind and Infinite Intelligence. It is the intermediary through which we may draw on the forces of Infinite Intelligence at will. It alone contains the secret process by which mental impulses are modified and changed into their spiritual equivalent—and the medium through which prayer may be transmitted to the source capable of answering prayer.

The possibilities of creative effort connected with the subconscious mind are stupendous and imponderable. They inspire me with awe.

The subconscious mind is more susceptible to influence by impulses of thought mixed with "feeling" or emotion than by those originating solely in the reasoning portion of the mind. In fact, there is evidence to support the theory that ONLY emotionalized thoughts have any ACTION influence on the subconscious mind. Emotion rules the majority of people. If it is true that the subconscious mind responds more quickly to and is influenced more readily by thought impulses well mixed with emotion, it is essential to realize the importance of emotions.

There are seven major positive emotions and seven major negative emotions. The negatives voluntarily inject themselves into the thought impulses that ensure passage into the subconscious mind. The positives must be injected through the principle of auto-suggestion, into the thought impulses we want to pass on to our subconscious mind. (Instructions given in Step 3, auto-suggestion.)

Seven major positive emotions:

- DESIRE

- FAITH

- LOVE

- SEX

- ENTHUSIASM

- ROMANCE

- HOPE

There are other positive emotions, but these are the seven most powerful, and the ones most commonly used in creative effort. Master these seven emotions by USING them and the other positive emotions will be at your command when you need them. Remember that in this context, you are studying a book intended to help you develop a "money consciousness" by filling your mind with positive emotions. We do not become money conscious by filling our mind with negative emotions.

Seven major negative emotions to be avoided:

- FEAR

- JEALOUSY

- HATRED

- REVENGE

- GREED

- SUPERSTITION

- ANGER

Positive and negative emotions cannot occupy the mind at the same time. One or the other must dominate. It is your responsibility to *make sure that positive emotions constitute the dominating influence of your mind.* Here the law of HABIT will come to your aid. Form the habit of applying and using the positive emotions! Eventually, they will dominate your mind so completely that the negatives cannot enter it.

What reason have we to believe that this same energy does not connect every human brain with Infinite Intelligence? There are no tollgates between the human finite mind and Infinite Intelligence. Communication costs nothing except patience, faith, persistence, understanding, and a SINCERE DESIRE to communicate. Moreover, the approach can be made only by each individual. You either go direct or you do not communicate.

The subconscious mind is the intermediary that translates our prayers into what Infinite Intelligence can recognize, presents the message, and brings back the answer in the form of a definite plan or idea for procuring the object of the prayer. Understand this principle and you will know why mere words read from a prayer book cannot and will never serve as an intermediary.

I believe that before your prayer will reach Infinite Intelligence, it is probably transformed from its original thought vibration into terms of spiritual vibration. Faith is the only known agency which will give your thoughts a spiritual nature. FAITH and FEAR make poor bedfellows. Where one is found, the other cannot exist.

THE BRAIN

The Broadcasting and Receiving Station for Thought

The Creative Imagination is the "receiving set" of the brain; it receives thoughts released by the brains of others. It is the agency of communication between our conscious, or reasoning, mind and the four sources from which we may receive thought stimuli.

When stimulated, or "stepped up" to a high rate of vibration, the mind becomes more receptive to the vibration of thought, which reaches it through the ether from outside sources. This "stepping up" process takes place through positive or negative emotions. Through emotions, the vibrations of thought may be increased.

Vibrations of an exceedingly high rate are the only vibrations picked up and carried by the ether from one brain to another. Thought is energy traveling at an exceedingly high rate of vibration. Thought, which has been modified or "stepped up" by any of the major emotions, vibrates at a much higher rate than ordinary thought, and it is this type of thought which passes from one brain to another, through the broadcasting machinery of the human brain.

As previously noted, the emotion of sex is at the top of the list of human emotions as far as intensity and driving force are concerned. The brain that has been stimulated by the emotion of sex vibrates at a much more rapid rate than it does when that emotion is quiescent or absent.

The result of sex transmutation is the increase of the rate of vibration of thoughts to such a pitch that the Creative Imagination becomes highly receptive to ideas, which it picks up from the ether. On the other hand, when the brain is vibrating at a rapid rate, it not only attracts thoughts and ideas released by other brains through the medium of the ether, but it gives to our own thoughts that "feeling," which is essential before those thoughts will be picked up and acted on by our subconscious mind.

Thus, you will see that the broadcasting principle is the factor through which you mix feeling, or emotion, with your thoughts and pass them on to your subconscious mind. The subconscious mind is the "sending station" of the brain, through which vibrations of thought are broadcast. The Creative Imagination is the "receiving set," through which the vibrations of thought are picked up from the ether.

Along with the important factors of the subconscious mind and the faculty of the Creative Imagination, which constitute the sending and receiving sets of your mental broadcasting machinery, consider now the principle of auto-suggestion, which is the medium by which you may put into operation your "broadcasting" station.

Through the instructions described in Step 3, auto-suggestion, you were informed of the method by which DESIRE may be transmuted into its monetary equivalent. Operation of your mental "broadcasting" station is a comparatively simple procedure. There are three principles to bear in mind and to apply when you wish to use your broadcasting station—the SUBCON-SCIOUS MIND, CREATIVE IMAGINATION, and AUTO-SUGGESTION. The stimuli through which you put these three principles into action have been described—the procedure begins with DESIRE.

The greatest forces are intangible.

Through past ages, humans have depended too much on physical senses, which has limited our knowledge to physical things that we could see, touch, weigh, and measure.

We are now entering the most marvelous of all ages—an age that will teach us something of the intangible forces of the world about us. Perhaps we shall learn, as we pass through this age, that the "other self" is more powerful than the physical self we see when we look into a mirror.

Sometimes we speak lightly of the intangibles—the things we cannot perceive through any of our five senses; when we hear them, it should remind us that we are all controlled by forces that are unseen and intangible.

The whole of humankind has not the power to cope with nor to control the intangible force wrapped up in the rolling waves of the oceans. Humankind has not the capacity to understand the intangible force of gravity, which keeps this little earth suspended in midair, and keeps us from falling from it, much less the power to control that force. Humans are entirely subservient to the intangible force that comes with a thunderstorm, and just as helpless in the presence of the intangible force of electricity—we really don't even know what electricity is, where it comes from, or what is its purpose!

This by any means is not the end of our ignorance in connection with things unseen and intangible. We don't understand the intangible force and intelligence wrapped up in the soil of the earth—the force that provides our every morsel of food we eat, every article of clothing we wear, every dollar we carry in our pockets.

THE SIXTH SENSE

The Door to the Temple of Wisdom

The SIXTH SENSE is the portion of the sub-conscious mind referred to as the Creative Imagination. It has also been referred to as the "receiving set" through which ideas, plans, and thoughts flash into our mind. The "flashes" are sometimes called "hunches" or "inspirations."

The sixth sense defies description! It cannot be described to anyone who has not mastered the other principles of this philosophy, because they have no knowledge and no comparison in experience. Understanding the sixth sense comes only by meditation through mind development from within. The sixth sense is perhaps the medium of contact between the human finite mind and Infinite Intelligence, a mixture of the mental and the spiritual.

After you have mastered the thirteen principles described in this abridged book and more thoroughly described in the original book, you will be prepared to accept as truth a statement that would have been incredible to you, namely: Through the aid of the sixth sense, you will be warned of impending dangers in time to avoid them, and notified of opportunities in time to embrace them. A "guardian angel" comes to your aid and to do your bidding with the development of the sixth sense—a "guardian angel" who opens to you at all times the door to wisdom.

The sixth sense comes as near to being a miracle as anything I have ever experienced; it appears so only because I don't understand the principle's method of operation.

This much I do know—there is a power or a First Cause or an Intelligence that permeates every atom of matter and embraces every unit of perceptible energy. This Infinite Intelligence converts acorns into oak trees, causes water to flow downhill in response to the law of gravity, follows night with day, and winter with summer, each maintaining its proper place and relationship to the other.

This Intelligence may, through these principles, be induced to aid in transmuting DESIRES into concrete or material form. I have this knowledge because I have experimented with it—and have EXPERIENCED IT.

Step by step, you have been led to this, the last principle. If you have mastered each of the preceding principles, you are now prepared to accept, without being skeptical, the stupendous claims made here. If you have not mastered the other principles, you must do so before you may determine, definitely, whether or not the claims made in this Step are fact or fiction.

Being an earnest student of psychology, I knew, of course, that all people have become what they are because of their DOMINATING

THOUGHTS and DESIRES. I knew that every deeply seated desire has the effect of causing us to seek outward expression so that desire could be transmuted into reality. And I knew that self-suggestion builds character.

Somewhere in the cell structure of the brain is an organ that receives vibrations of thought ordinarily called "hunches." Science has not discovered where this organ of the sixth sense is located, but the fact remains that human beings *do* receive accurate knowledge through sources other than the physical senses. Such knowledge, generally, is received when the mind is under the influence of extraordinary stimulation.

Any emergency that arouses emotions and causes the heart to beat more rapidly than normal may, and generally does, bring the sixth sense into action. Anyone who has experienced a near accident while driving knows that the sixth sense often comes to our rescue and aids, by split seconds, in avoiding the accident.

The sixth sense cannot be taken off and put on at will. Ability to use this great power comes slowly, through application of the other principles.

The sixth-sense Step is included for the purpose of presenting a complete philosophy so you may unerringly guide yourself in attaining whatever you ask of life. The starting point of all achievement is DESIRE. The finishing point is the KNOWLEDGE that leads to understanding—understanding of self, others, the laws of Nature, recognition and understanding of HAPPINESS.

This sort of understanding comes in its fullness only through familiarity with and use of the principle of the sixth sense, hence that principle had to be included as part of this Law of Success philosophy, for the benefit of those who demand more than money.

I encourage you to reread this book again, or purchase the original book, and eventually you will find yourself in possession of a power that enables you to throw off discouragement, master fear, overcome procrastination, and draw freely on your imagination. Then you will feel the touch of that unknown "something" that has moved the spirit of every truly great thinker, leader, artist, musician, writer, businessperson, etc. Then you will be in a position to convert your DESIRES into their physical or financial counterpart.

Conclusion

SELF-ASSESSMENT INVENTORY

28 Important Questions to Answer About Yourself

Annual self-analysis is essential and should disclose a DECREASE IN FAULTS and an increase in VIRTUES. We either go ahead, stand still, or go backward in life. Our object should be, of course, to go ahead.

Your annual self-assessment should be made at the end of each year, so you can include in your New Year's Resolutions any improvements the analysis indicates should be made. Take this inventory by asking yourself the following questions, and by checking your answers with the aid of someone who will not permit you to deceive yourself as to their accuracy.

Personal Inventory Self-Analysis

1. Have I attained the goal I established as my objective for this past year? (You should work with a definite yearly objective as part of your major life objective.)

2. Have I delivered service of the best possible QUALITY, or could I have improved any part of this service?

3. Have I delivered service in the greatest possible QUANTITY?

4. Has the spirit of my conduct been harmonious and cooperative at all times?

5. Have I permitted the habit of PROCRASTINATION to decrease my efficiency? If so, to what extent?

6. Have I improved my PERSONALI-TY? If so, in what ways?

7. Have I been PERSISTENT in following my plans through to completion?

8. Have I reached DECISIONS PROMPTLY AND DEFINITELY on all occasions?

9. Have I permitted any fears to decrease my efficiency?

10. Have I been either over-cautious or under-cautious?

11. Has my relationship with my work associates been pleasant or unpleasant? If unpleasant, has the fault been partly or wholly mine?

12. Have I dissipated any of my energy through lack of CONCENTRATION of effort?

13. Have I been open-minded and tolerant in connection with all subjects?

14. In what way have I improved my ability to render service?

15. Have I been intemperate in any of my habits?

16. Have I expressed, either openly or secretly, any form of EGOTISM?

17. Has my conduct toward my associates caused them to RESPECT me?

18. Have my opinions and DECISIONS been based on guesswork or accuracy of analysis and THOUGHT?

19. Have I followed the habit of budgeting my time, my expenses, and my income?

20. How much time have I devoted to UNPROFITABLE effort?

21. How can I RE-BUDGET my time and change my habits to be more efficient?

22. Have I been guilty of any conduct not approved by my CONSCIENCE?

23. Have I rendered MORE SERVICE AND BETTER SERVICE than I was paid to render?

24. Have I been unfair to anyone? If so, in what way?

25. If I was the purchaser of my own services for the past year, would I be satisfied with my purchase?

26. Am I in the right vocation? If not, why not?

27 Have the purchasers of my services been satisfied? If not, why not?

28. What is my present rating on the fundamental principles of success? (Make this rating fairly and frankly, and have it checked by someone who is courageous enough to respond accurately.)

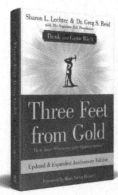